Frogs

Victoria Blakemore

For Mrs. Mendoza, my mentor and friend. I know how much you love frogs!

Copyright info/picture credits

Cover, Storyblocks; Page 3, Storyblocks; Page 5, Storyblocks; Page 7, Storyblocks; Page 9, Storyblocks; Pages 10-11, Story-blocks; Page 13, Cathy Keifer/AdobeStock; Page 15, Story-blocks; Page 17, Storyblocks; Page 19, Ivan Kuzmin/AdobeStock; Page 21, Alfonso1967/Pixabay; Page 23; Story-blocks; Page 25, Storyblocks; Page 27, Storyblocks; Page 29, Storyblocks; Page 31, Storyblocks; Page 33, Storyblocks

Table of Contents

What Are Frogs?

Frogs are amphibians. They start their lives in the water, then can live on land.

There are nearly 5,000 different kinds of frogs. They come in all different colors and sizes. They are found in most parts of the world.

Frogs are related to toads. They are both amphibians and members of the Anura order.

Size

Frogs come in many different sizes. Many frogs are between one and three inches long.

The largest kind of frog is the goliath frog. It can be about one foot long and weigh up to seven pounds.

Some frogs are very small.

There are some that are less

than an inch long.

Physical Characteristics

Frogs are **cold-blooded**. They need to spend time in the sun to heat up if they get too cold. They cool off in the water if they get too hot.

Frog eyes are large and bulge out of their head. They are able to see almost all the way around their body.

Some frogs can use the color of their skin as **camouflage**. They can blend in with their habitat.

Habitat

Frogs are often found around ponds, lakes, rivers, and marshes. They need areas that are warm and wet.

Many frogs live in rainforests. The **climate** there is very warm and humid.

Range

Frogs are found on every continent except Antarctica.

There are about ninety different kinds of frogs that live in the United States.

Diet

Frogs are **carnivores.** They eat only meat.

Their diet is made up of insects such as flies, mosquitos, moths, and grasshoppers. Some larger frogs also eat small snakes, mice, or other frogs.

They have a long, sticky tongue
that shoots out of their mouth
and wraps around their prey.

When a frog is hunting, it sits completely still, except for the blinking of its eyes. When prey gets close enough, it catches the prey with its long, sticky tongue.

Some frogs leap into the air to catch flying prey. Others may hide in the water to catch prey.

A frog's skin is **permeable**, which means that it can absorb water. Frogs get all of the water they need through their skin.

Communication

Frogs use sound, movement, and touch to communicate with each other.

Frogs have a special vocal sac in their neck. They push air through the sac to make croaking noises. Some frogs can also make whistling sounds.

Frogs can wave their arms or nod their heads to get the attention of other frogs.

Movement

Frogs have very strong back legs and webbed feet, both of which help them to be great jumpers.

They can move very quickly. Some can hop as fast as about ten miles per hour. This is very fast for an animal that is so small.

Many frogs can jump as far as twenty times their body length in one jump.

Frog Life Cycle

Frogs lay thousands of eggs at a time. They hatch into tadpoles. They have a big head, long tail, and no legs.

Tadpoles grow into froglets. They develop legs, but still have a long tail. Then, the frog's lungs grow, the tail shrinks, and the froglet becomes an adult frog.

A tadpole can also be called a

pollywog. Almost all tadpoles

live only in the water.

Frog Life

Frogs are usually **solitary**. They spend most of their time alone. Many are **nocturnal**. They are most active at night.

Some frogs **hibernate** during the winter. They find a safe place such as a hollow log and sleep through the colder weather.

Frogs can hibernate under the water. They can **absorb** oxygen through their skin.

Poisonous Frogs

Some kinds of frogs have skin that **secretes** poisonous **toxins**. Touching them can be deadly.

Frogs that are poisonous are often brightly colored. Their colors are a warning to predators that they are **toxic**.

The poison dart frog is one of

the most poisonous animals

on Earth.

Population

Most frog populations are **declining** each year. There are many frogs that are **endangered** and some that are already **extinct**.

Since frogs need wet climates to survive, they are **vulnerable** to habitat loss, pollution, and warming temperatures.

In the wild, frog life spans can range from a few months to years. It is hard for researchers to track frogs to know for sure.

Frogs in Danger

Frogs are facing many threats. Their habitats are being destroyed. **Pesticides** and other chemicals are causing many frogs to die.

Changing temperatures can make it hard for frogs to find areas that are wet enough to lay their eggs.

The chytrid fungus is making frogs

sick. It is spread when infected

frogs come into contact with

other frogs or their water sources. 29

Helping Frogs

People are trying to help frogs. They are working to prevent the spread of disease, protect habitats, and stop the use of harmful **pesticides**.

There are some places where conservation zones protect frog habitats. This provides them with a safe place to live.

In some places, amphibians are not allowed to be brought into the country. This is to try to prevent the spread of disease.

Some countries are banning the use of certain **pesticides**. They want to stop frog habitats from being polluted and keep frogs from dying.

Glossary

Absorb: to take in, soak up

Camouflage: using color to blend in to the surroundings

Carnivore: an animal that eats only meat

Climate: the usual weather in a certain area

Cold-Blooded: an animal whose temperature changes with the air temperature

Declining: getting smaller

Endangered: at risk of becoming extinct

Extinct: when there are no more of an animal left in the wild

Hibernate: when an animal sleeps through the winter

Nocturnal: animals that are active at night

Permeable: allowing liquids or gas to go through

Pesticides: chemicals used to kill insects that harm plants and crops

Secretes: producing a fluid and releasing it from the body

Solitary: living alone

Toxic: poisonous

Toxins: poisonous substances that are secreted by animals

Vulnerable: able to be hurt or injured

About the Author

Victoria Blakemore is a first grade

teacher in Southwest Florida with a

passion for reading.

You can visit her at

www.elementaryexplorers.com

Also in This Series

Gray Wolves — Victoria Blakemore
Sloths — Victoria Blakemore
Flamingos — Victoria Blakemore
Camels — Victoria Blakemore
Koalas — Victoria Blakemore
Honey Bees — Victoria Blakemore
Pandas — Victoria Blakemore

Pangolins — Victoria Blakemore
White-Tailed Deer — Victoria Blakemore
Orcas — Victoria Blakemore
Giraffes — Victoria Blakemore
Corn — Victoria Blakemore
Meerkats — Victoria Blakemore
Echidnas — Victoria Blakemore

Walruses — Victoria Blakemore
Raccoons — Victoria Blakemore
Bald Eagles — Victoria Blakemore
Apples — Victoria Blakemore
Arctic Foxes — Victoria Blakemore
Red Pandas — Victoria Blakemore
Cassowaries — Victoria Blakemore

Tigers — Victoria Blakemore
Ladybugs — Victoria Blakemore
Moose — Victoria Blakemore
Beluga Whales — Victoria Blakemore
Leopards — Victoria Blakemore
Elephants — Victoria Blakemore
Jellyfish — Victoria Blakemore

Binturongs — Victoria Blakemore
Lions — Victoria Blakemore
Dolphins — Victoria Blakemore
Reindeer — Victoria Blakemore
Hammerhead Sharks — Victoria Blakemore
Hippos — Victoria Blakemore
Pumpkins — Victoria Blakemore

Peafowl — Victoria Blakemore
Chameleons — Victoria Blakemore
Florida Panthers — Victoria Blakemore
Aye-Ayes — Victoria Blakemore
Black Bears — Victoria Blakemore
Cheetahs — Victoria Blakemore
Manatees — Victoria Blakemore

Gingerbread — Victoria Blakemore
Polar Bears — Victoria Blakemore
Hot Chocolate — Victoria Blakemore
Orangutans — Victoria Blakemore
Coyotes — Victoria Blakemore
Marshmallows — Victoria Blakemore
Strawberries — Victoria Blakemore

Also in This Series

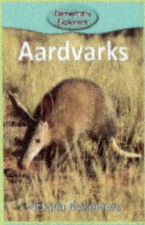

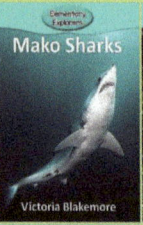

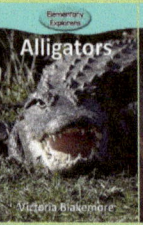

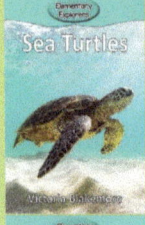

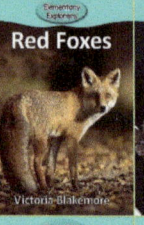

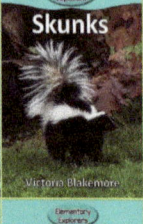

Aardvarks	Mako Sharks	Alligators	Frogs	Hedgehogs	Brown Bears	Bongos
Sea Turtles	Quokkas	Muskrats	Zebras	Red Foxes	Ring-Tailed Lemurs	Platypuses
Anteaters	Kangaroos	Rhinos	Jaguars	Wombats	Capybaras	Gorillas
Cats	Skunks	Butterflies	Dingoes	Snow Leopards	African Wild Dogs	Penguins
Whale Sharks	Wolverines	Warthogs	Caracals	Badgers	Seals	Hummingbirds
Pikas	Humpback Whales	Pumas	Lemonade	Llamas	Tulips	Ostriches
Sunflowers	Fennec Foxes	Sea Lions	Squirrels	Roses	Porcupines	Ice Cream

Victoria Blakemore

www.ingramcontent.com/pod-product-compliance
Lightning Source LLC
Chambersburg PA
CBHW051251020426
42333CB00025B/3161